The Travel Edition

Written and illustrated by
Rachel Caro

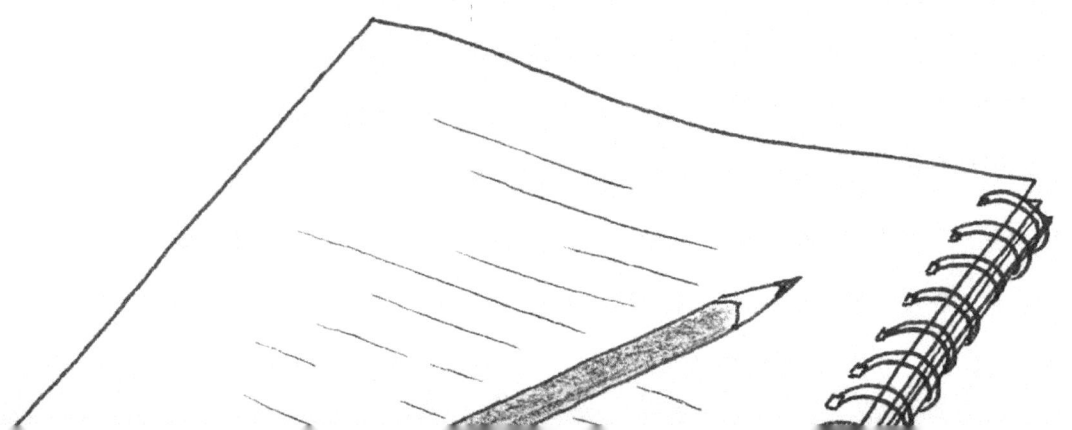

Text, illustrations, and educational material © 2016 Rachel Caro

First published in 2016 by Lava Press

Illustrations were done in pen and ink and charcoal

ISBN-10: 0-692-63476-2

ISBN-13: 978-0-692-63476-9

Printed and bound in the U.S.A.

Exploration of a

Coloring Storybook

At the end of this book you will find

ideas for taking your reading adventure farther:

Create.

Discover.

Dream.

Explore your world!

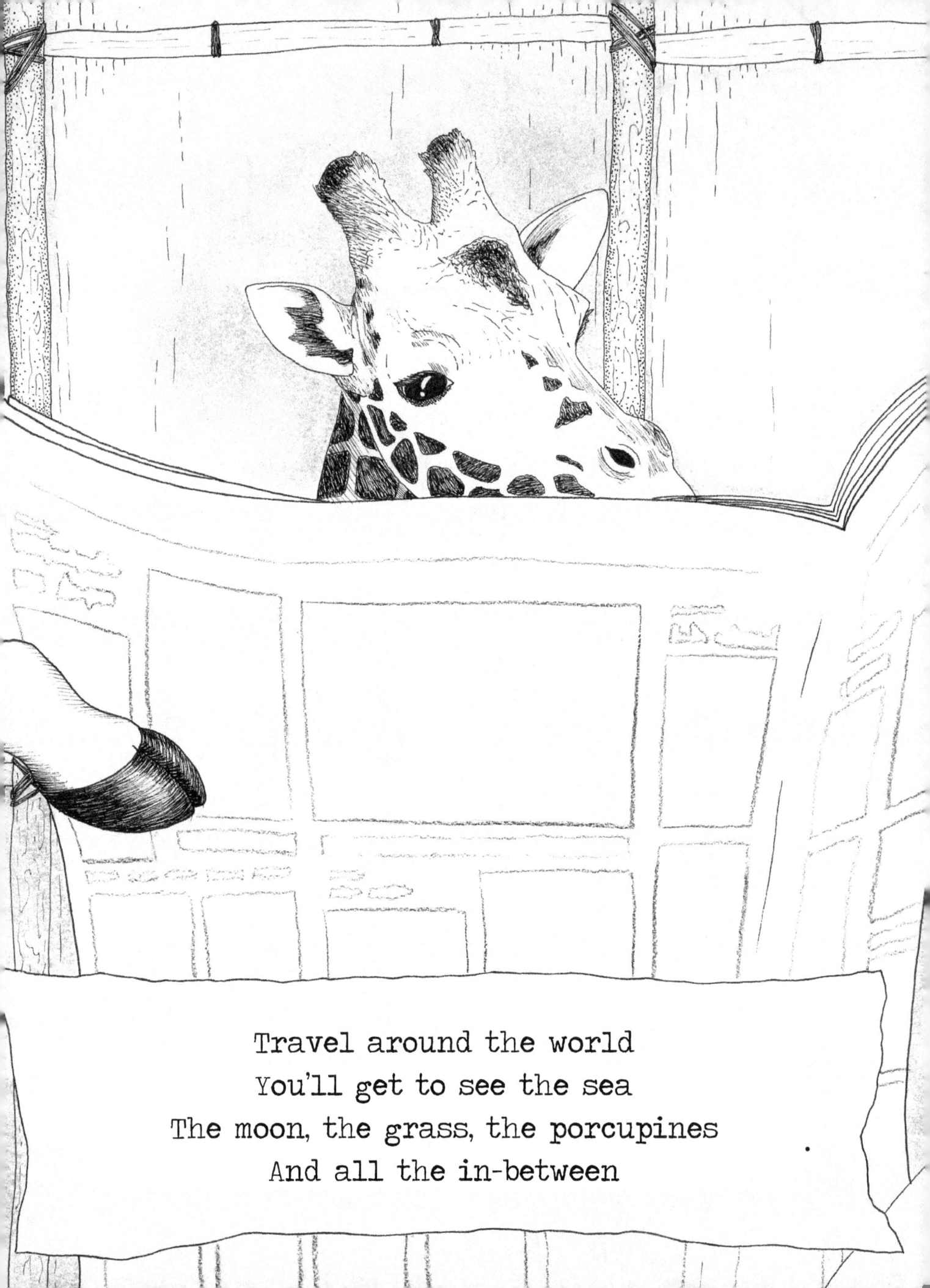

Travel around the world
You'll get to see the sea
The moon, the grass, the porcupines
And all the in-between

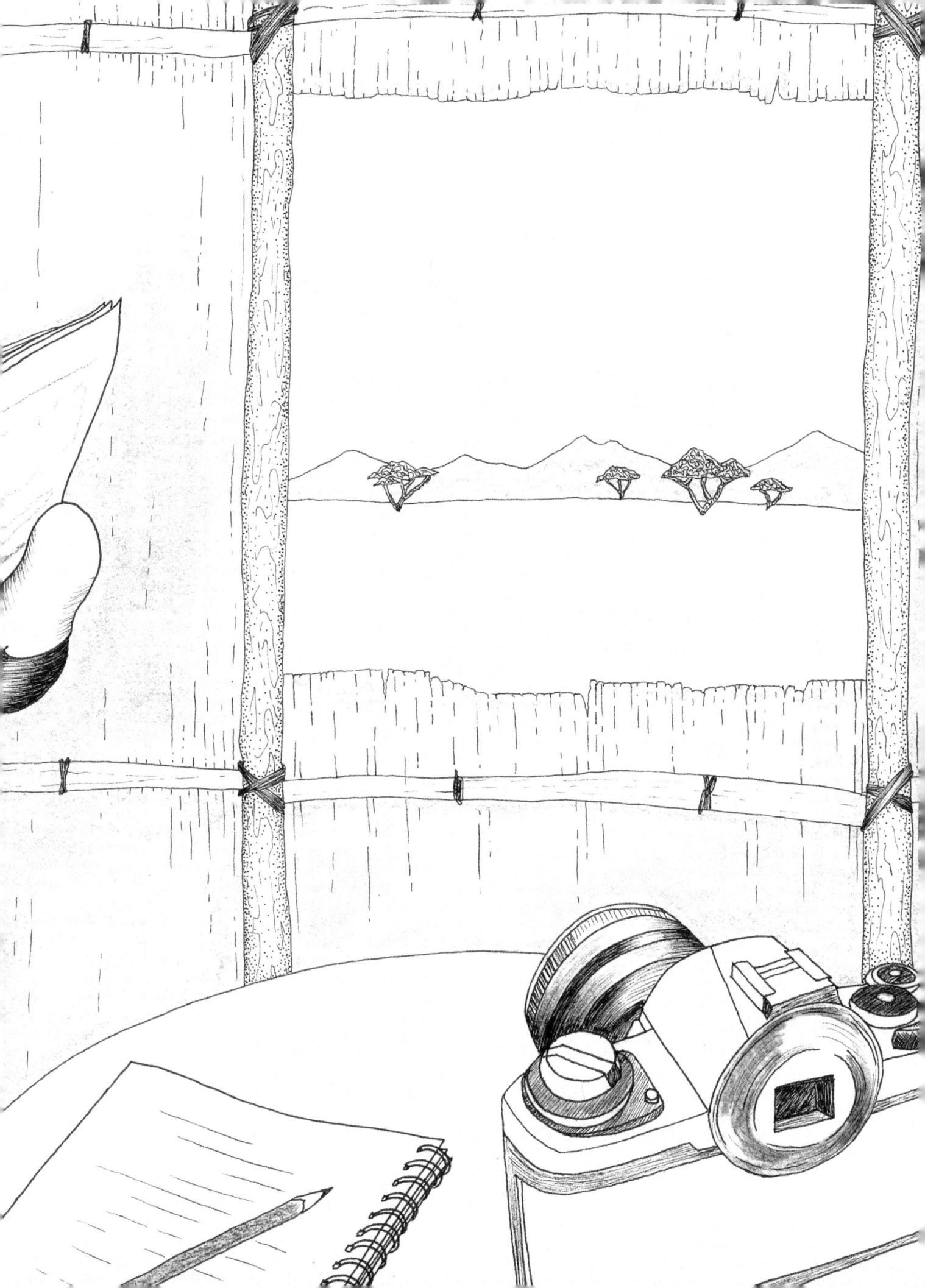

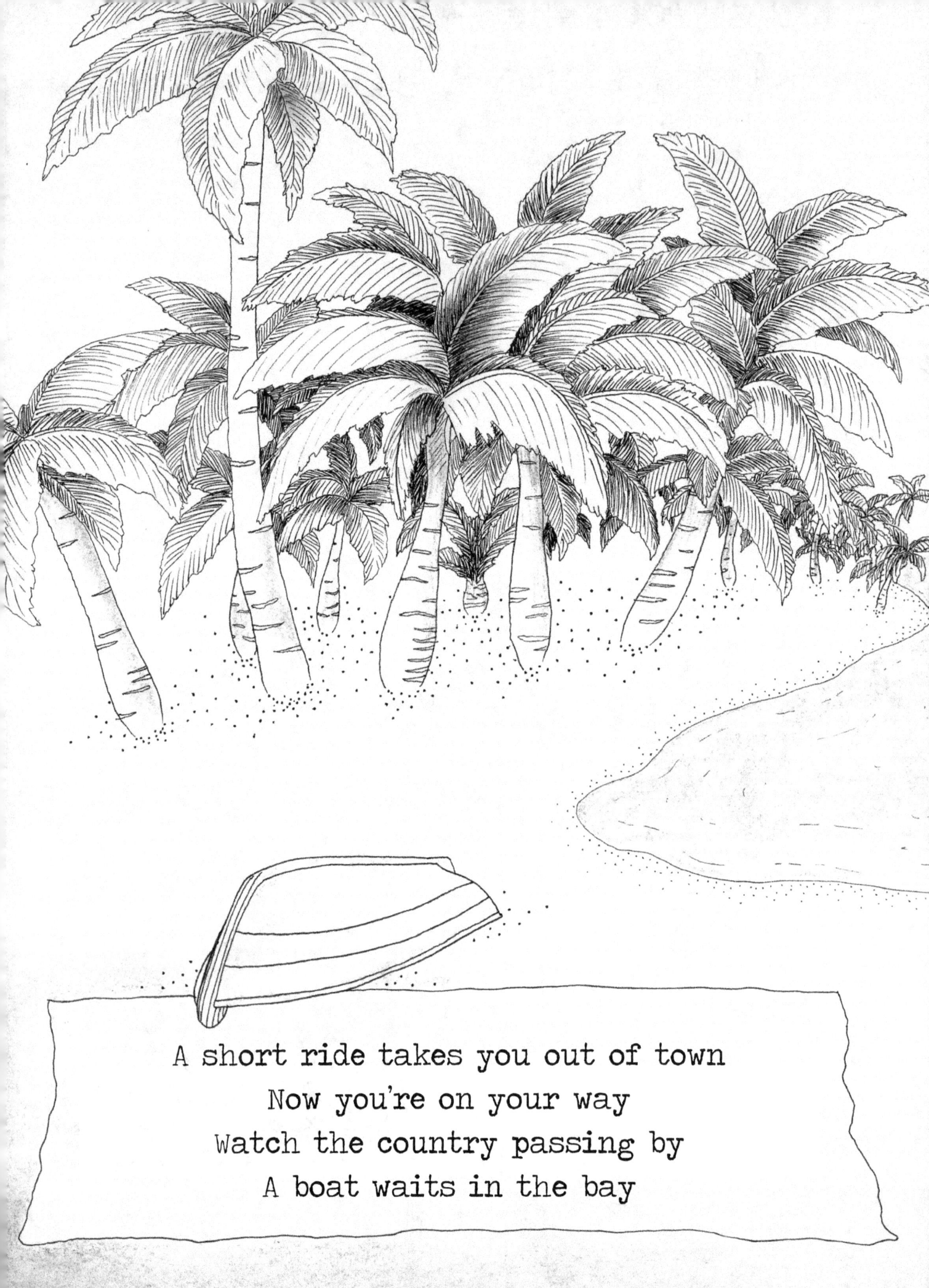

A short ride takes you out of town
Now you're on your way
Watch the country passing by
A boat waits in the bay

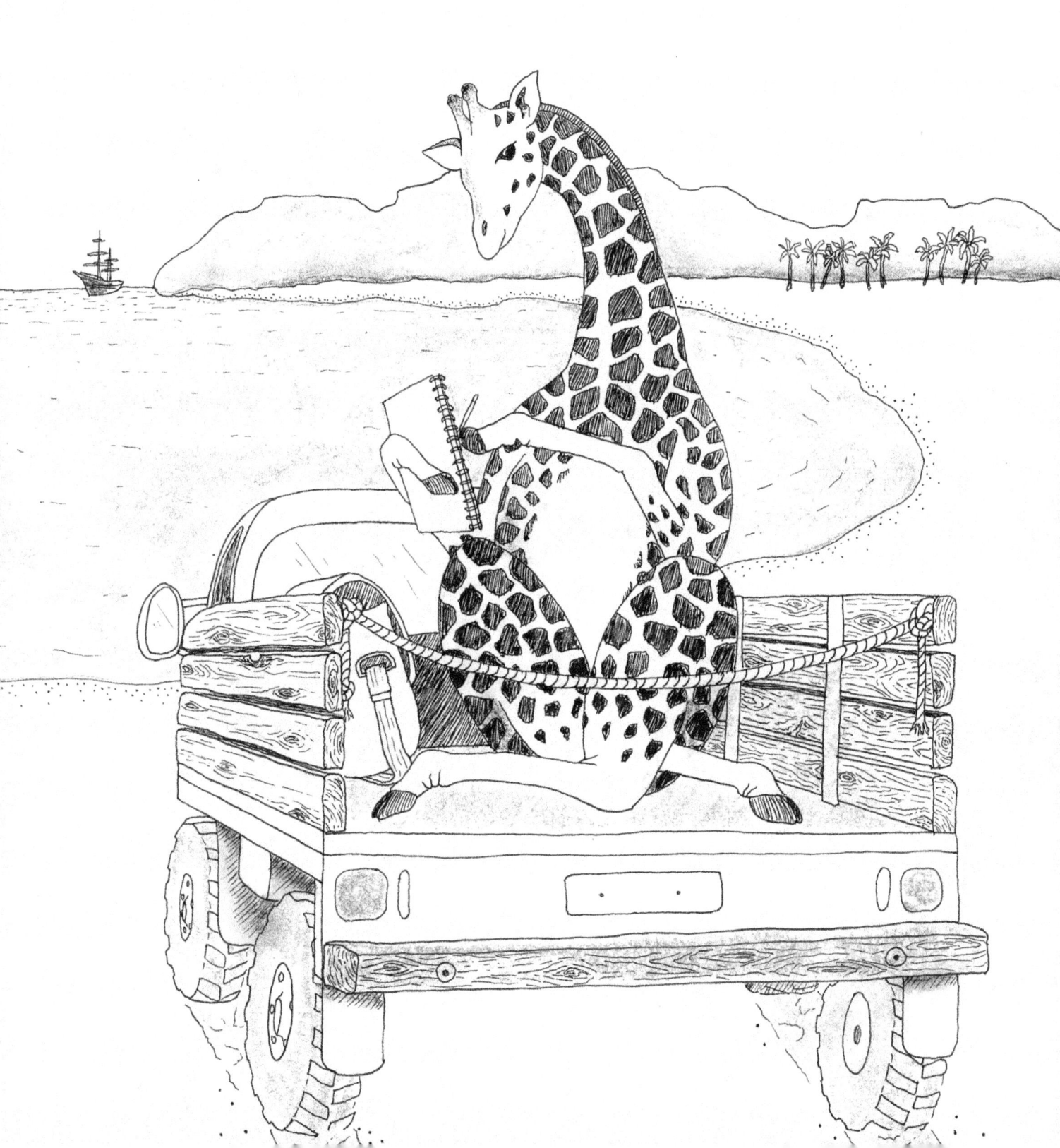

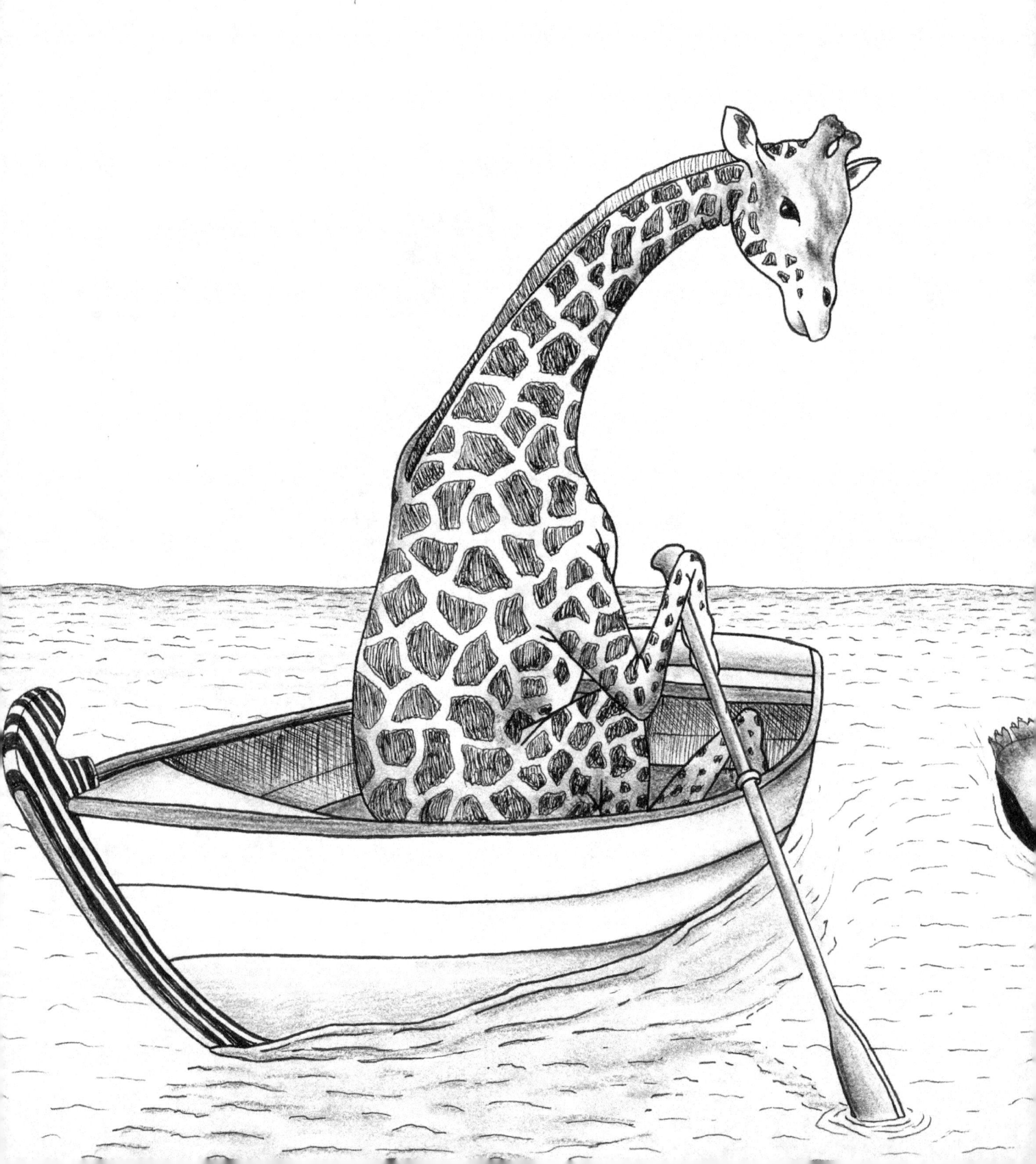

Sail the ocean westward
Finding islands in the cold
Where synchronized Gentoo penguins
Perform down below

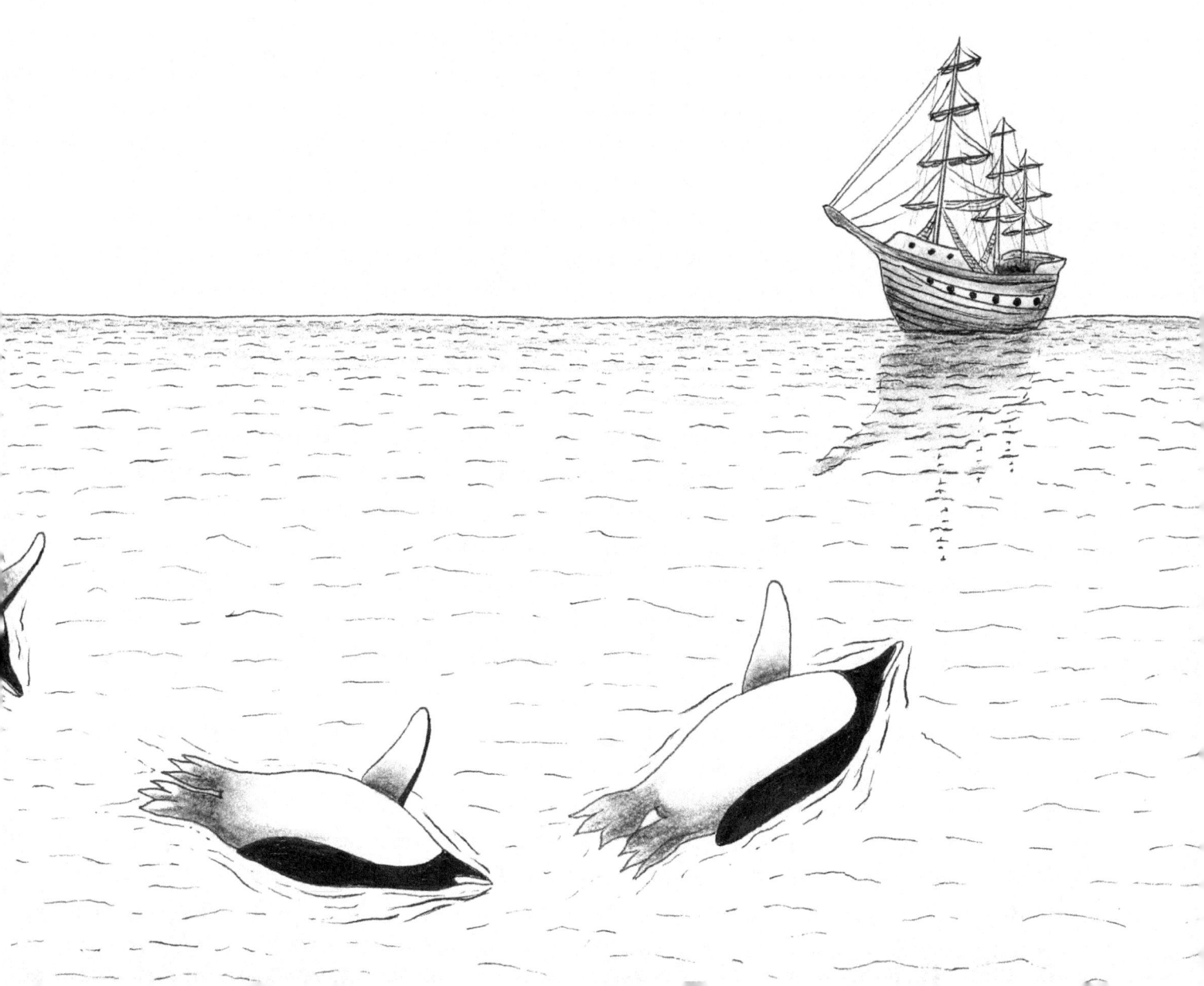

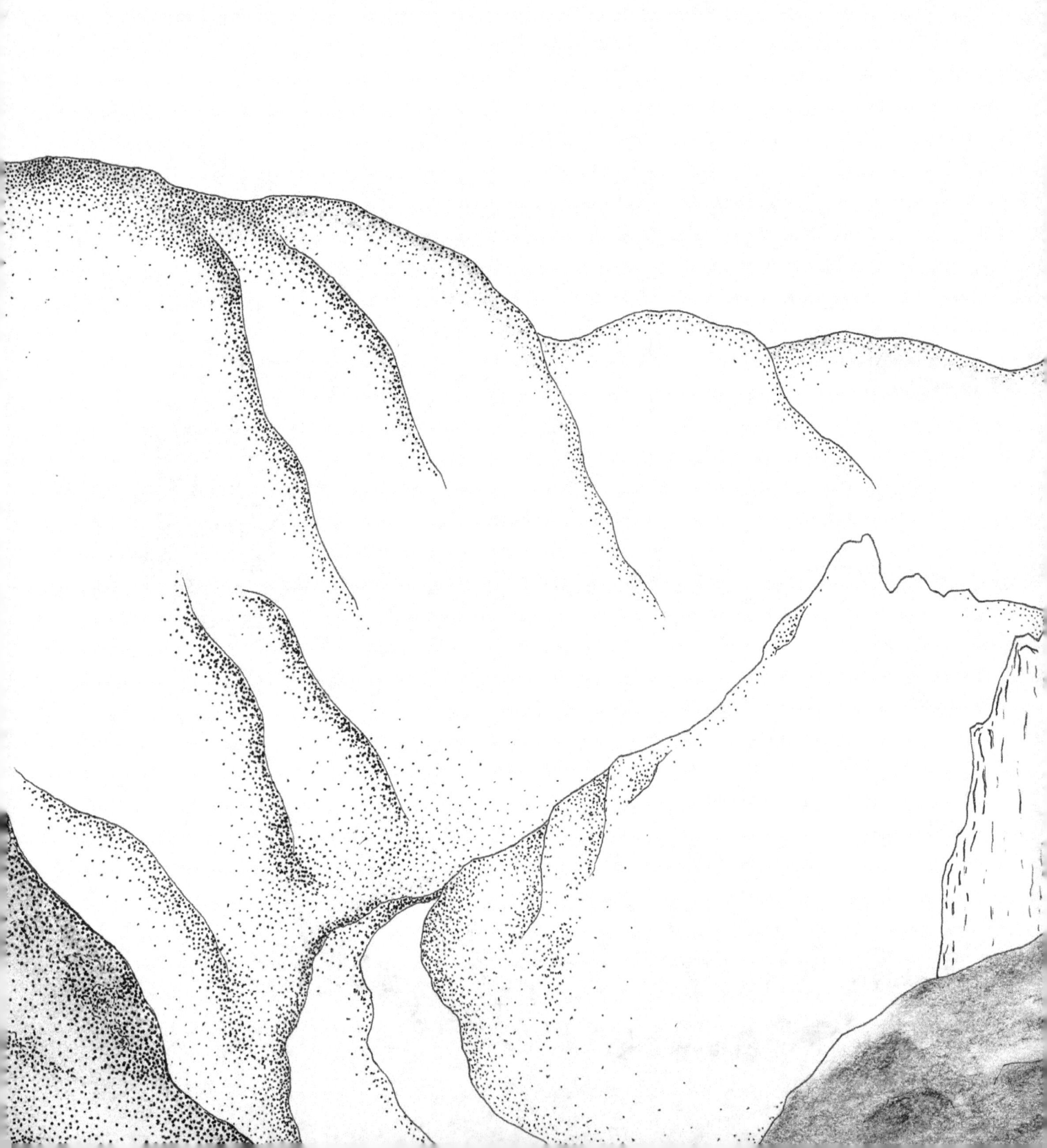

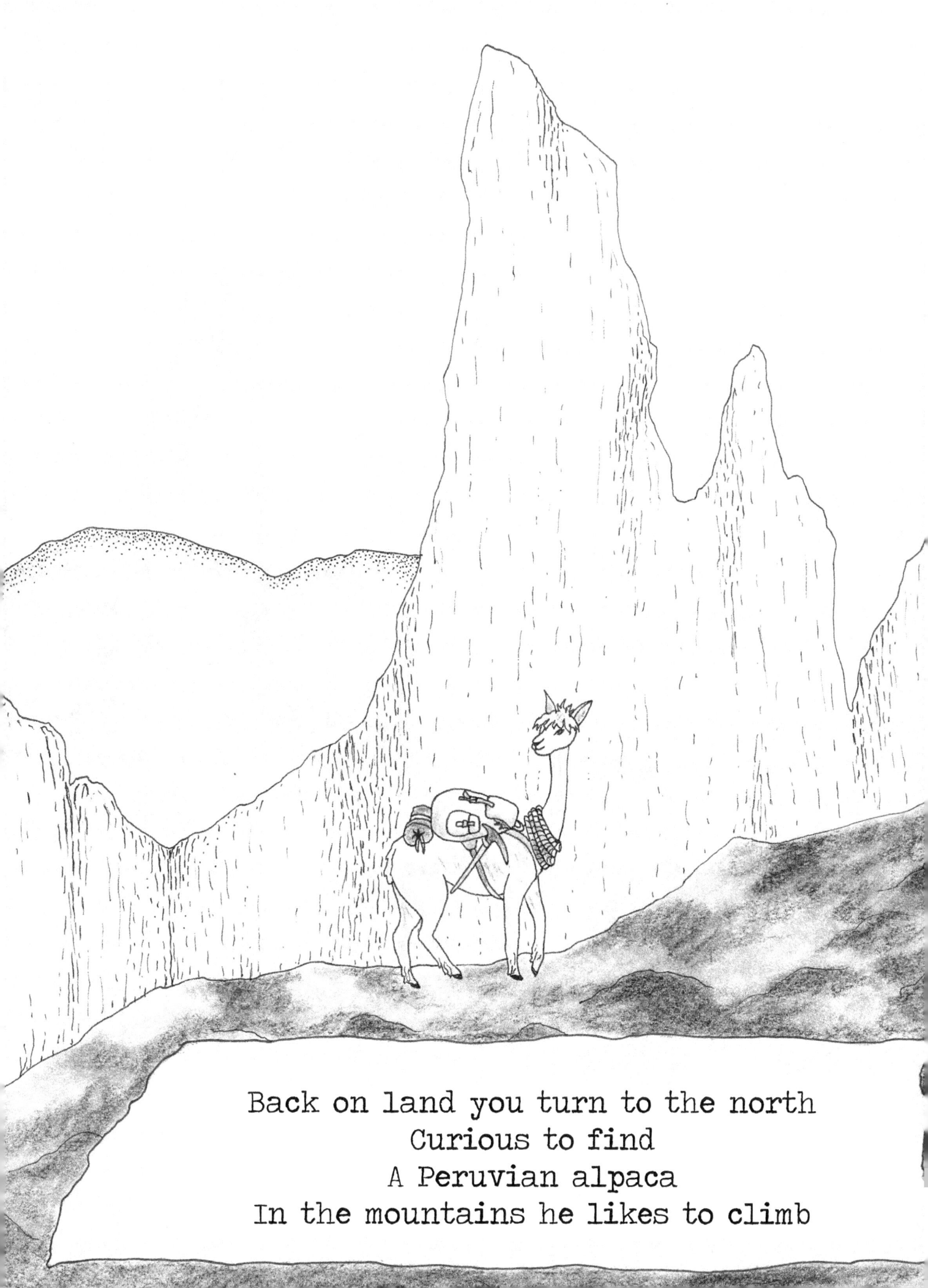

Back on land you turn to the north
Curious to find
A Peruvian alpaca
In the mountains he likes to climb

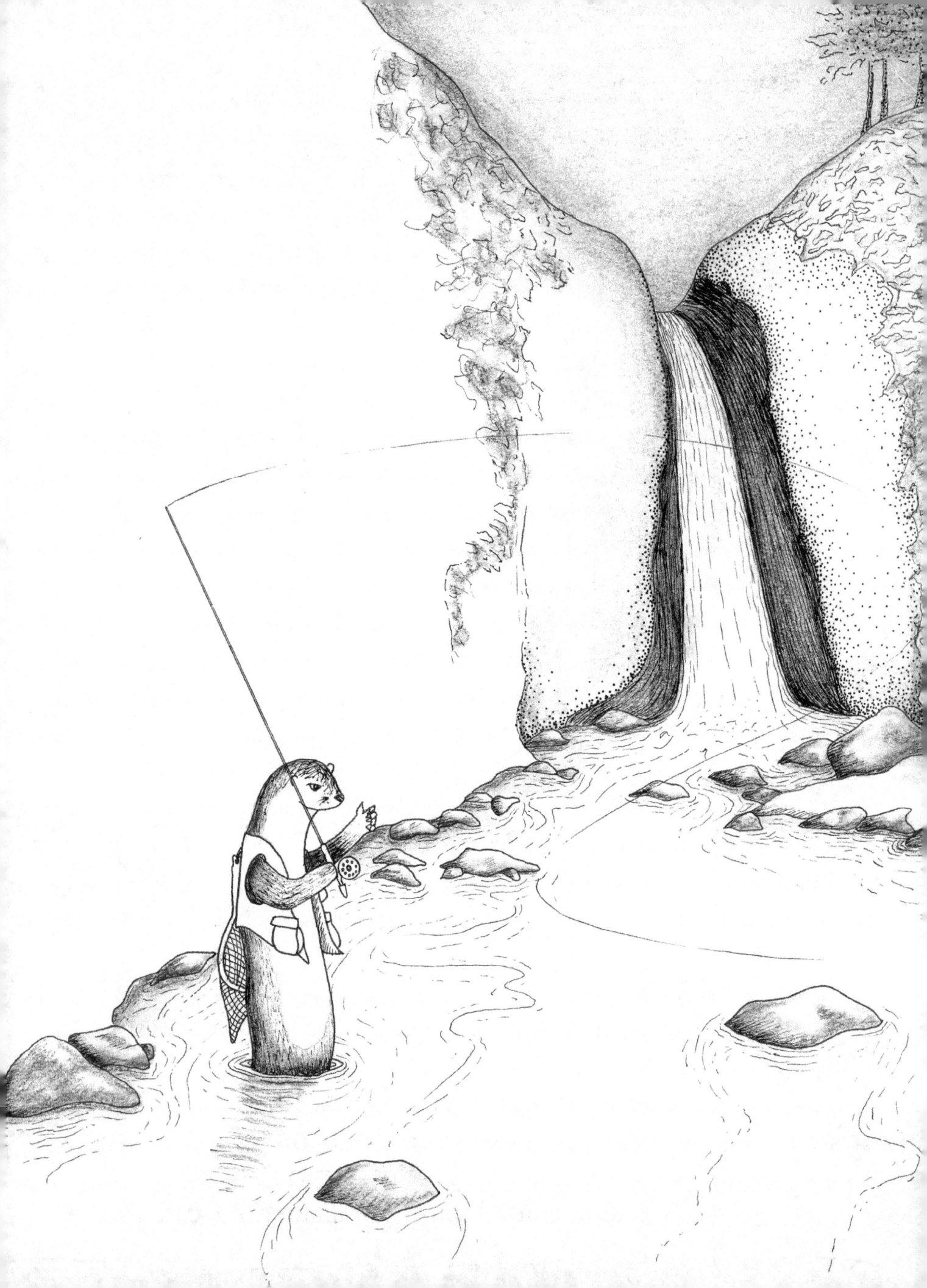

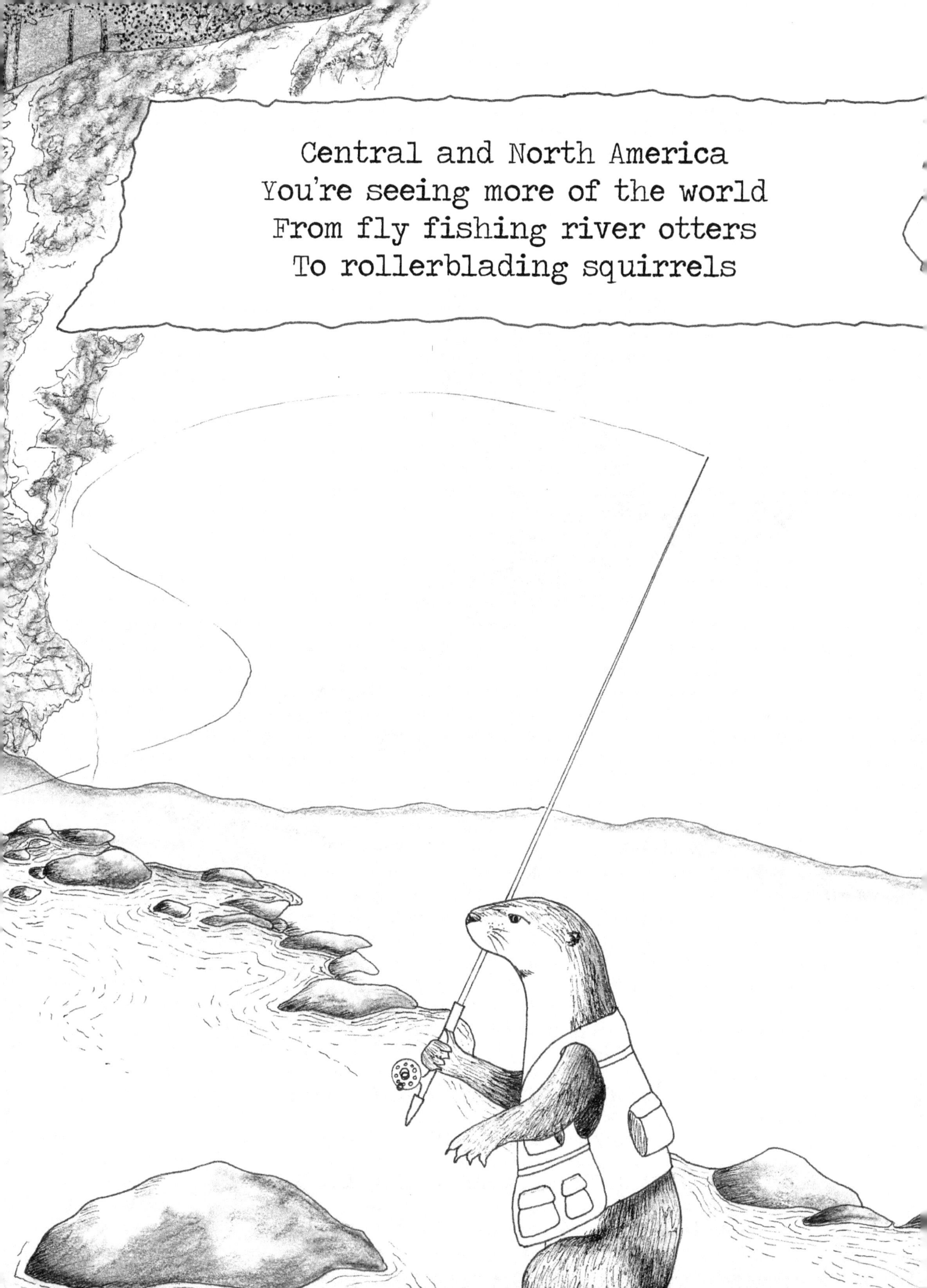

Central and North America
You're seeing more of the world
From fly fishing river otters
To rollerblading squirrels

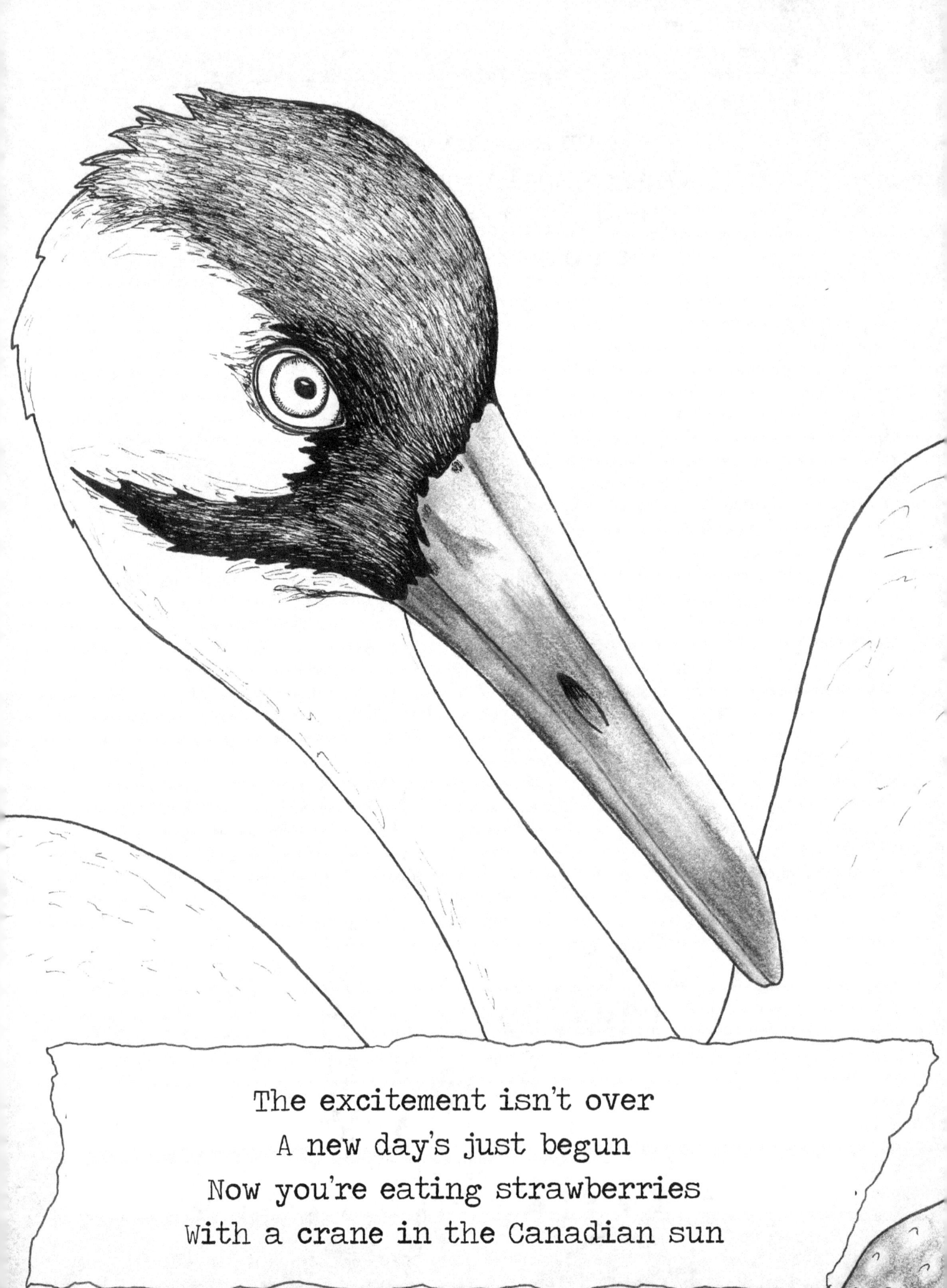

The excitement isn't over
A new day's just begun
Now you're eating strawberries
With a crane in the Canadian sun

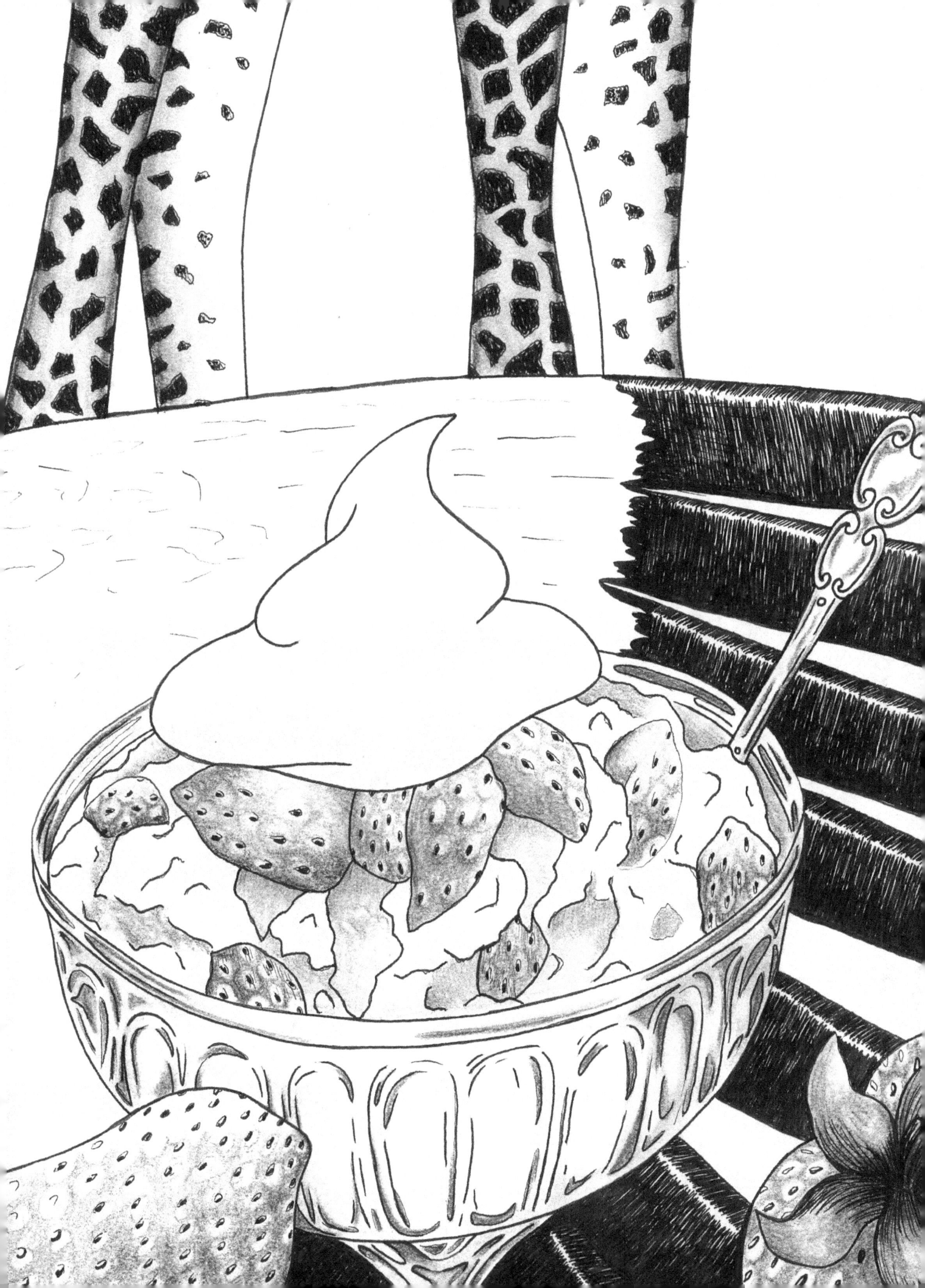

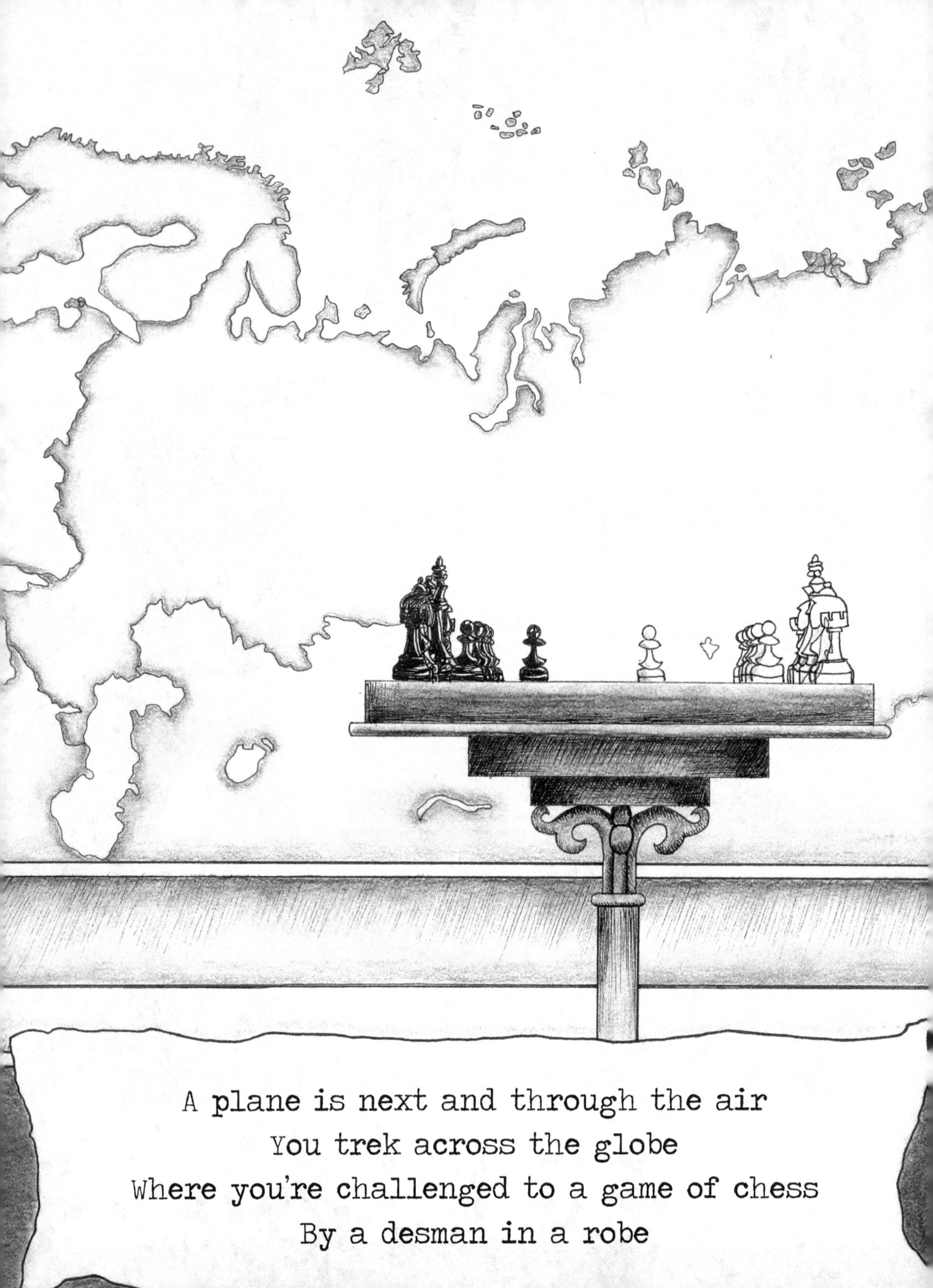

A plane is next and through the air
You trek across the globe
Where you're challenged to a game of chess
By a desman in a robe

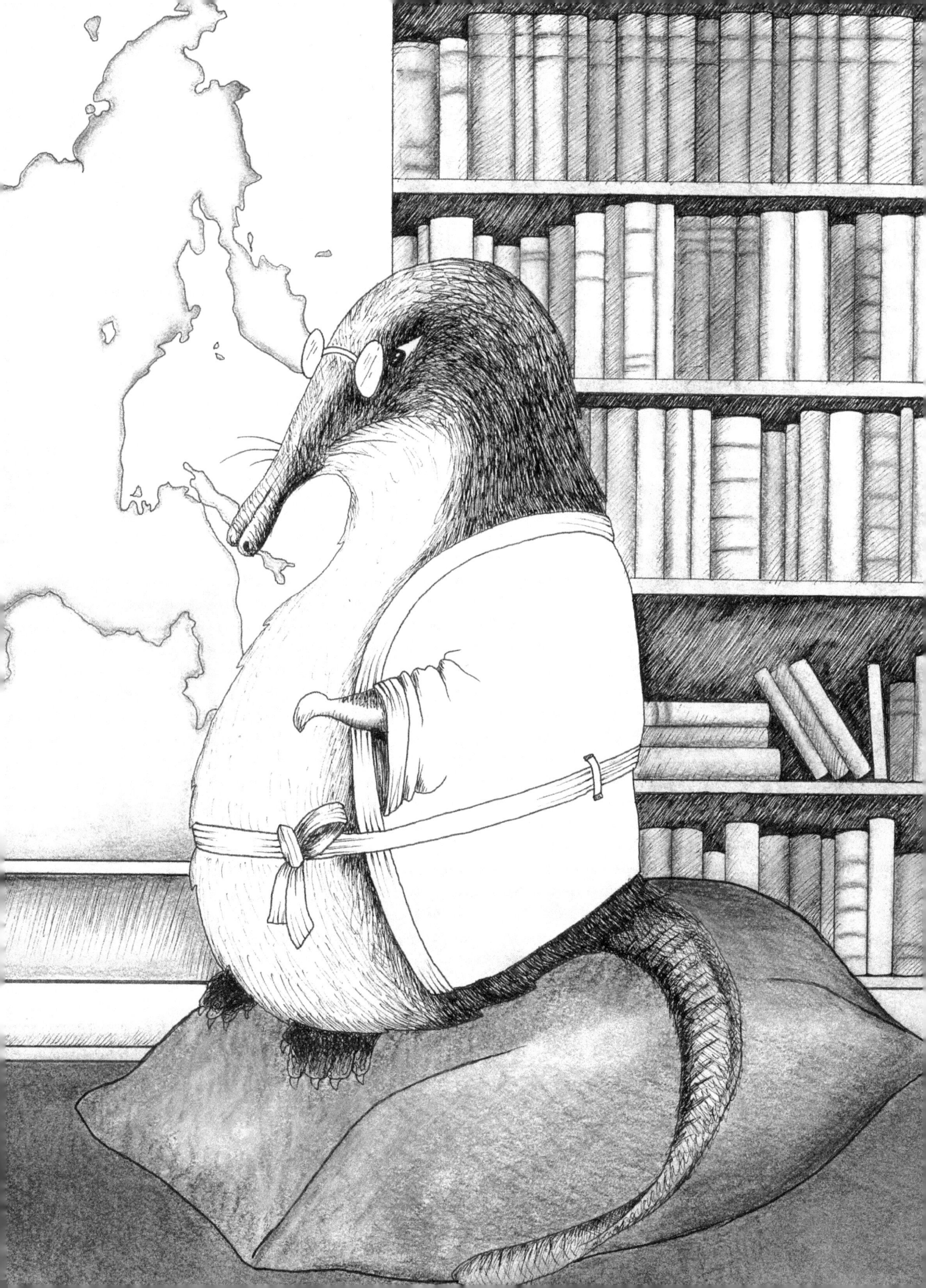

Southward bound on a train
From plateaus and Indian lace
To badminton-playing elephants
Impressive with their grace

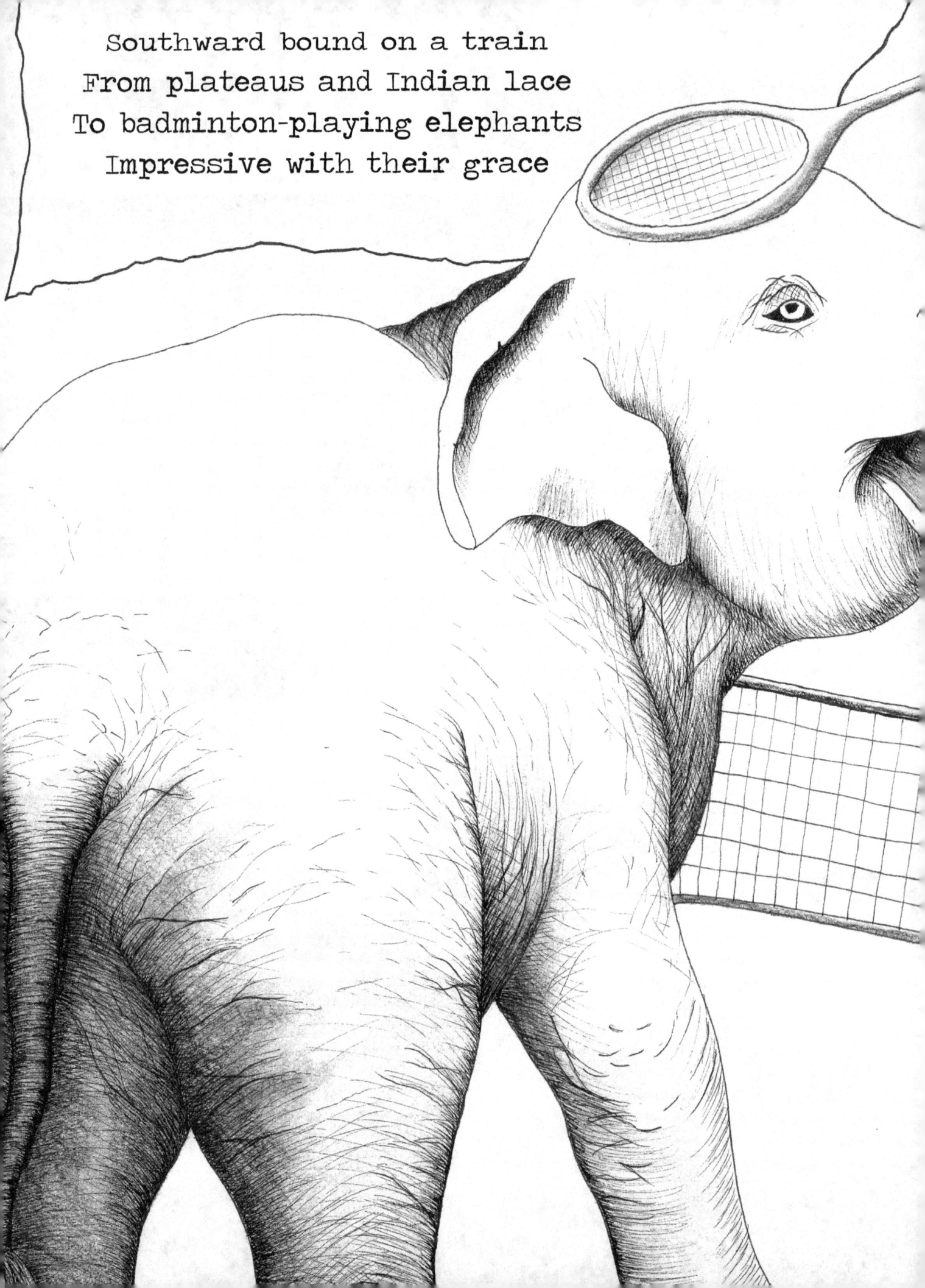

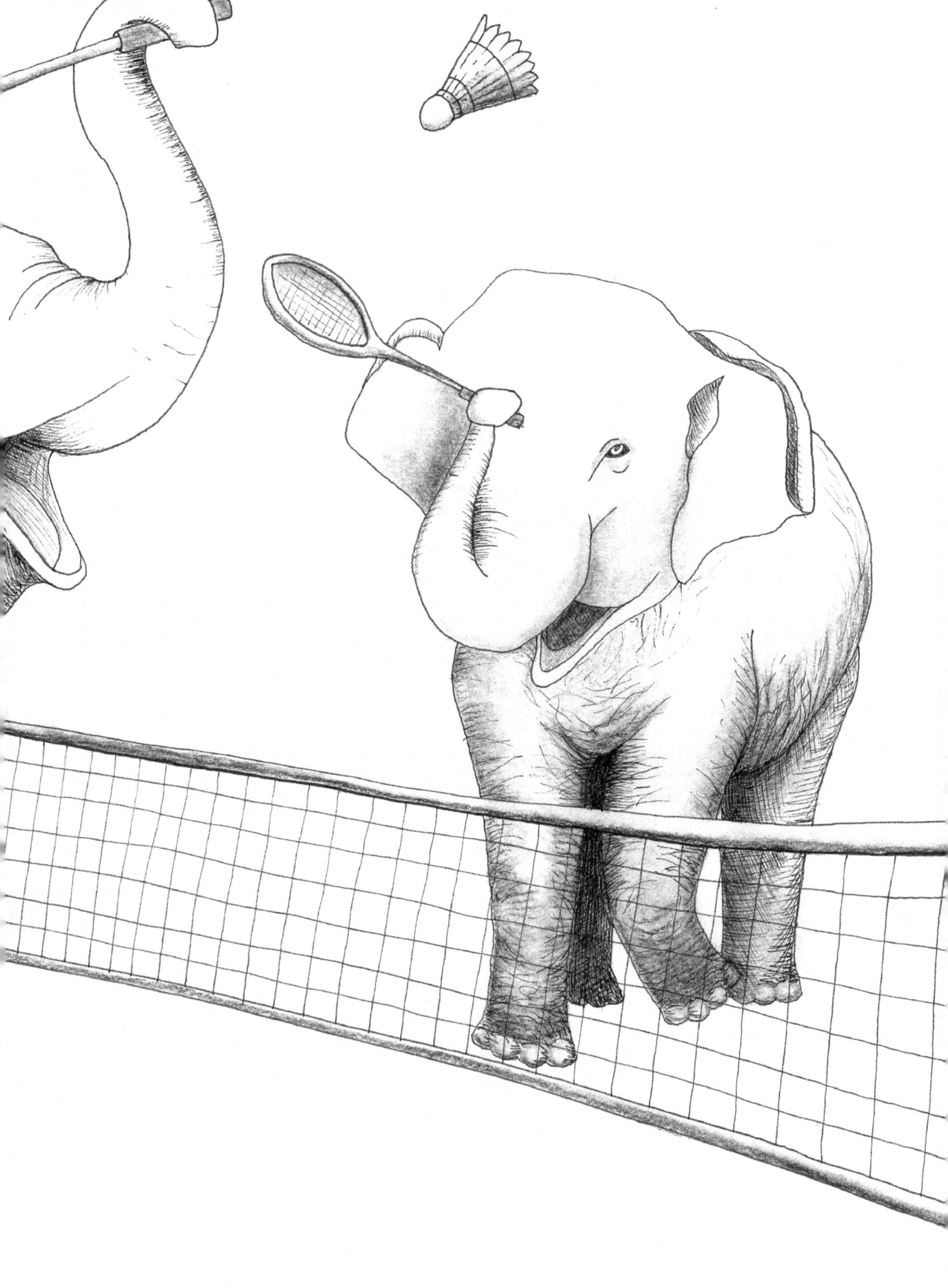

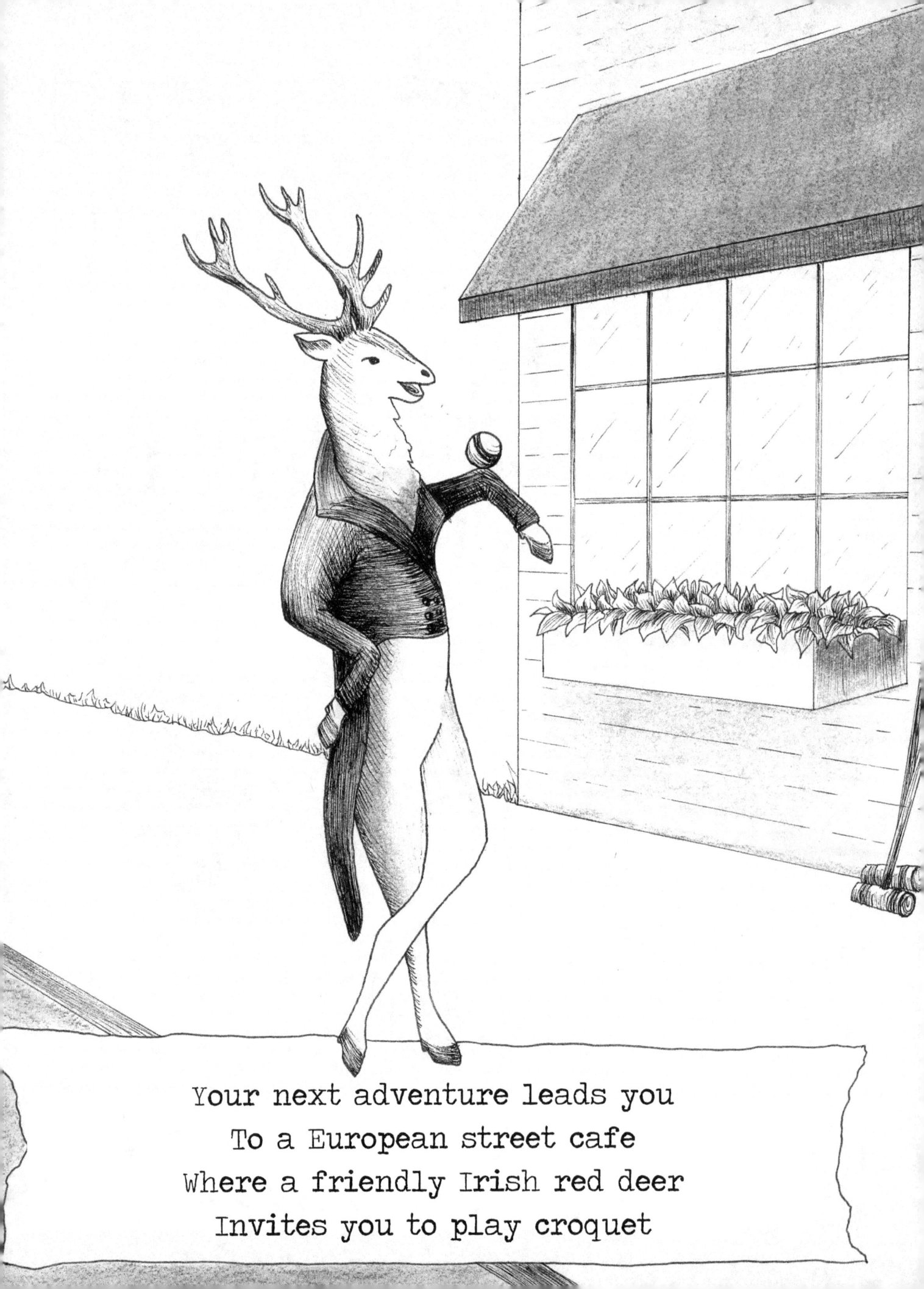

Your next adventure leads you
To a European street cafe
Where a friendly Irish red deer
Invites you to play croquet

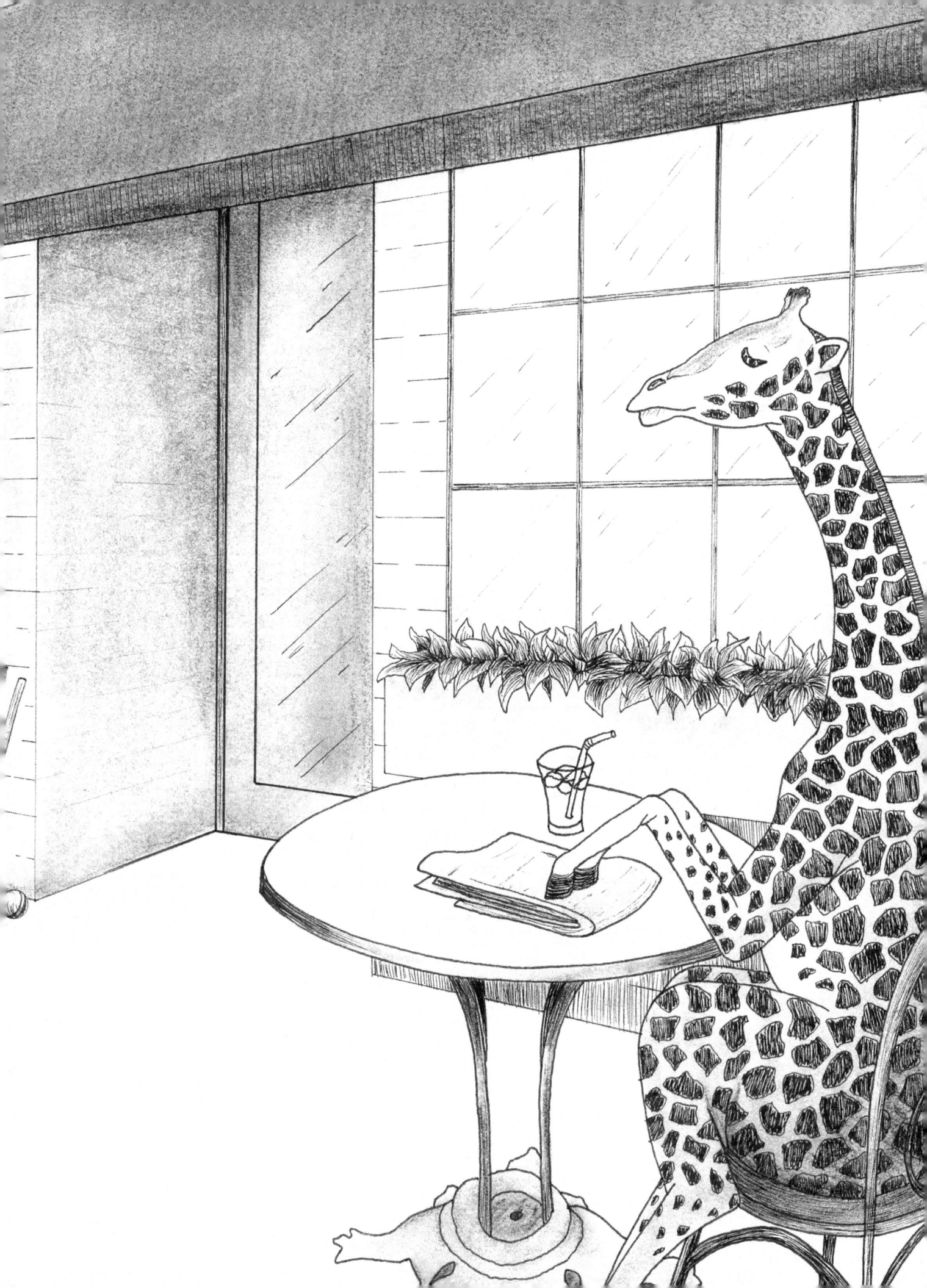

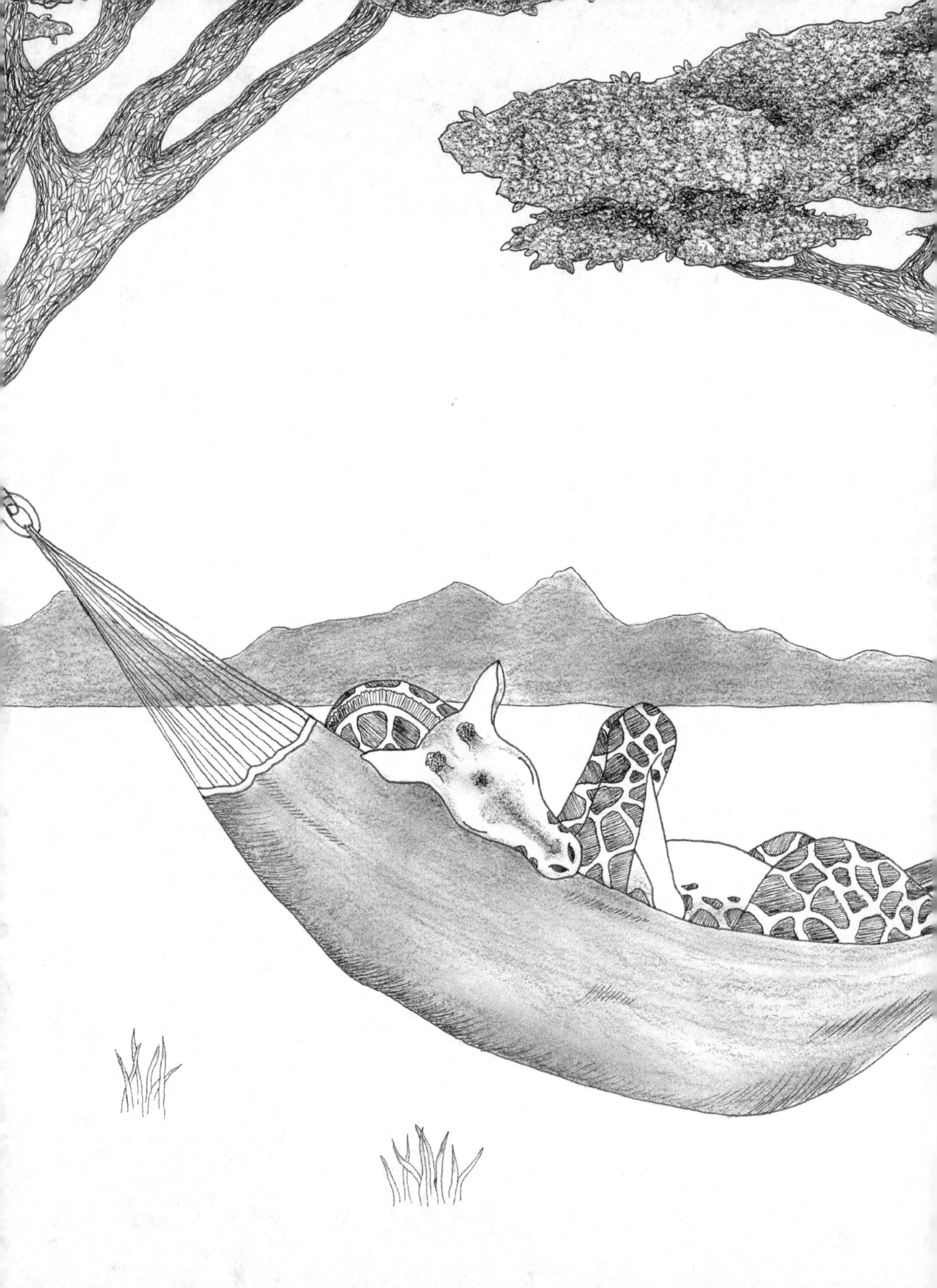

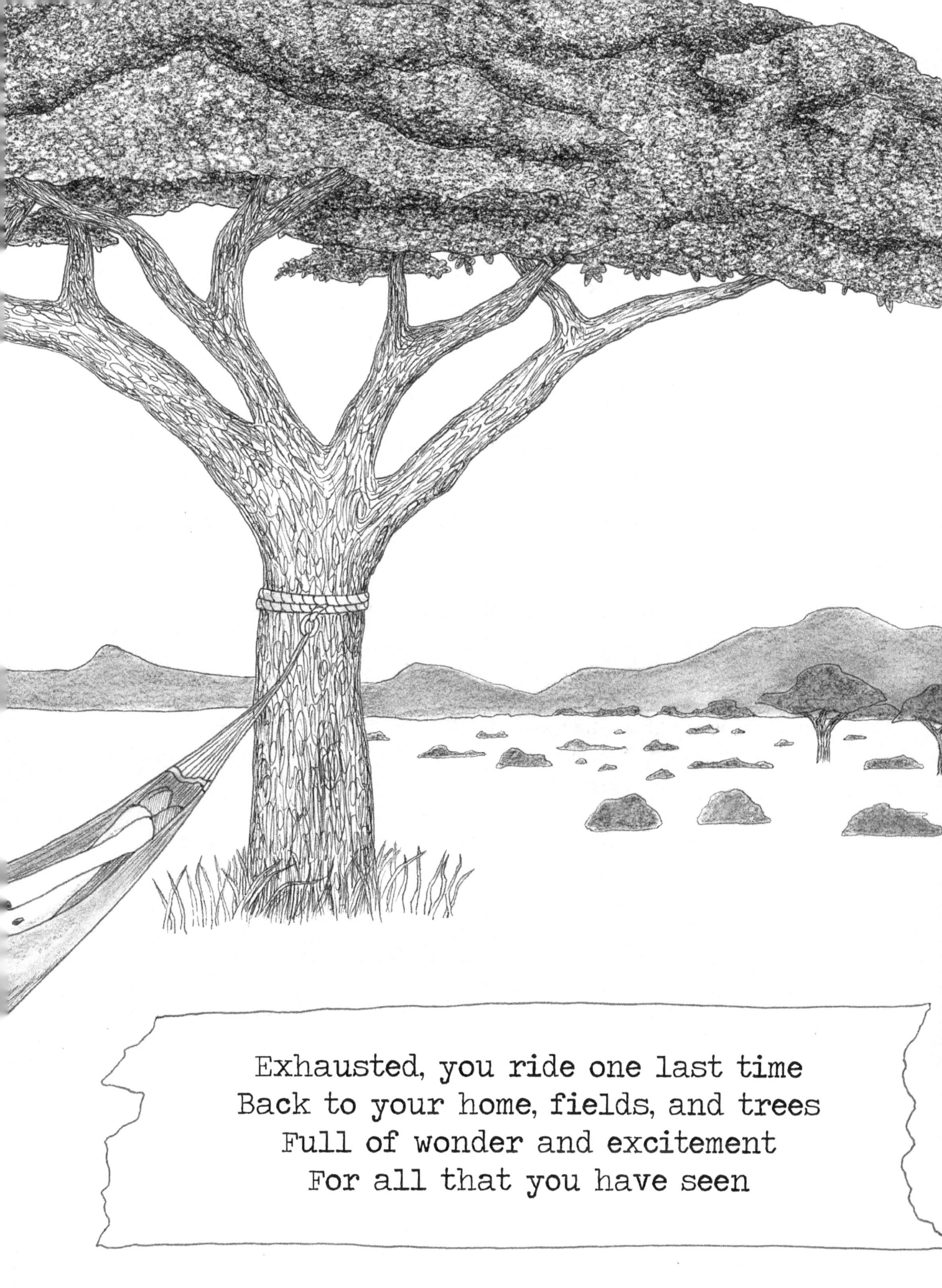

Exhausted, you ride one last time
Back to your home, fields, and trees
Full of wonder and excitement
For all that you have seen

Exploration of a
Coloring Storybook

Level 1

. . . for young children and their caregivers . . .

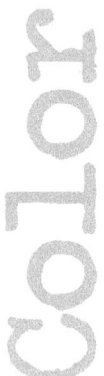

Color the pages of this book.

This book is full of different animals doing different activities. **Draw** your favorite animal doing your favorite activity.

"Read" this book to someone, making up a new story as you go along.

Pick a new **word** from this book and ask someone what it means.

Have someone help you follow the giraffe's journey on a **map**. From Africa, he travels west to the Falkland Islands, up through the Americas, across to Russia, down to India, and finally to Europe before returning to Africa.

When you look at the map, find out which **directions** are north, south, east, and west.

Take an imaginary **journey**!
- Choose one place in this book and pretend that you are going to take a trip there.
- Use other books to help you find out what kinds of things you can see and do there.
- Make a list of things you would need to pack for your journey.
- Draw a picture of you and your family on your traveling adventure.

Level 2

... for ages 8+ ...

Color the pages of this book using realistic or abstract color choices.

Read one page of this book and create your own **illustration** to go along with it using ink and charcoal or any other media.

Choose an illustration and **write** your own story to describe what is happening in the scene.

Go out and take **photographs** of the natural environment, and then **write** a journal entry about what you have seen.

Find any **words** throughout the story that may be unfamiliar. Look up these new words in a dictionary.

Construct a **map** of the world that shows the route the giraffe took on his journey, or construct a map of where you live

The giraffe, neotropical otters, whooping crane, Russian desman, Asian elephants, and red deer are all considered **endangered** species, with the Gentoo penguins listed as near-threatened. Find out what it means for an animal to be "endangered" or "threatened".

In this story we come across synchronized swimming, mountaineering, fly fishing, rollerblading, chess, badminton, and croquet. Are any of these **activities** available near you?

Carefully **observe** the illustrations and story again. **Analyze** the information for comprehension and further discussion.

- **Page 1-2**: What can we learn about the giraffe by looking at his surroundings? Can we tell where he lives or what he likes to do?

- **Page 3-4**: What is the giraffe doing in the truck? How can the giraffe reach the ship?

- **Page 5-6**: What helps penguins to swim or live in a cold climate? What is meant by the "islands in the cold"?

- **Page 7-8**: What is an alpaca? Do they really climb mountains?

- **Page 9-10**: What do river otters do with the fish they catch?

- **Page11-12**: Why do we only see the giraffe's legs in this illustration?

- **Page13-14**: What is a desman? What can we learn about him based on his feet, nose, and tail?

- **Page15-16**: How can we figure out what kind of elephants these are?

- **Page17-18**: What is croquet? Do you think this game was new to the giraffe?

- **Page19-20**: Where is the giraffe's home? Did he really take a trip around the world, or was it only a dream?

- **Bonus:** This journey sets sail through the eyes of a giraffe, who is awkward in his height and stature. He has to fold himself up to fit in the truck and dinghy, as well as other modes of transportation. He also had to make friends with others that were very different from himself. What can we learn from the challenges the giraffe has faced?

Plan a **trip** to a foreign place! Find the travel section of your local newspaper and choose a place to visit based on what you've read.

- **Geography:** Where in the world is it? Construct a map of your destination that includes physical and cultural features.

- **Language**: What language(s) do the people speak? Write out and translate some important phrases that you may use while traveling to this area.

- **Science**: What will the weather be like when you go on your trip? What types of animals live there?

- **Culture**: What types of food do the locals eat? What kinds of clothes do they wear? What are the houses like? What else is unique about their culture?

- **World news**: Find out more about why your place of interest was in the news.

- **History**: What historical landmarks can you see when you visit? What historical events took place in this area?

- **Physical fitness**: What activities will you participate in while you're visiting? What sports do the children and adults play?

- **Math:** How much would your trip cost? Consider transportation, lodging, food, activities, and souvenirs.

- **Arts**: Perform a dance or make a craft that is unique to your area of interest.

- **Creative writing**: Imagine that you really took a week-long trip. Write a "travel journal" of your experiences.

Level 3

. . . for young adults and adults . . .

Create a comfortable personal **environment** in your bedroom, living room, porch, or even your spare closet. Collect some paper and whatever art supplies you have lying around. Get cozy!

Color the pages of this book using realistic or abstract color choices, if desired.

The images in this book are only one version of how the written story can be expressed. If inspired, read one page of this book and create your own **illustration** to go with it.

These illustrations were drawn using ink and charcoal. Try creating any element of this book using other **mediums**.

The illustrator for this book used thick lines, thin lines, and even dots to communicate depth and texture. Pay attention to how the shadows of the palm trees and elephants are expressed by drawing lines closer together, while light areas are achieved by drawing lines farther apart. Notice how the strawberries are darker and seeded while the whipped cream is smooth. **Experiment** with similar techniques for shading and communicating texture.

Write a journal entry about something that happened in your life today. Even if you've not yet left this space or encountered any other "characters", you can describe the room and the way the air makes the curtains move. You can describe the flickering of the candle's flame or the way your new environment makes you feel.

Create

Write

Take an *actual* **trip**! Maybe you've traveled internationally before. Maybe you've never left your state. Either way, there are places you've not yet seen and experiences you've not yet ventured. Your final challenge is to plan a trip . . . and make it happen.

- **Location:** Where have you always wanted to go? What have you always wanted to see or do?

- **Timing**: How much time will you need for your trip? Do you have pre-planned vacation days, or can you go any time of the year? If traveling internationally, a destination's "shoulder season" typically offers the best balance of price and weather.

- **Points of interest**: What natural, cultural, or historical attractions are available? What recreational activities are available? What could you try that you've never done before?

- **Lodging:** Where will you stay? In a hostel, campground, hotel, or bed & breakfast? There may also be farm stays, work stays, or ecotourism opportunities available, if you'd like to enhance your experience.

- **Culture**: What types of foods should you try (or avoid)? Are there any cultural or religious considerations for clothing or behavior? What else is unique about the culture in this region?

- **World news**: Find out what's happening in your place of interest.

- **Expenses**: Consider transportation, lodging, food, attractions, and souvenirs. Will you also need a passport or to order local currency?

- **Do it**: Take a camera, keep a journal, and expect the unexpected. *Explore your world.*